TRUCKING IS A MAN'S JOB...

SAYS WHO?

Lyrical Press LLC

PO Box 620128

Charlotte, NC 28262

https://youtu.be/Jpkg07NNtL8

Printed in the United States of America

First printing, February 2021

Cover Designer by Rica Cabrex

ISBN 978-1-7364032-0-4

To Kwabena...My Dear Love

Many people often wonder why is it so "easy" to die, because sometimes it is too challenging to live!

Our Truckers

Traveling from state to state while diving into new adventures, truck drivers are highly needed yet unappreciated and overworked. As soon as the pandemic hit, WHO did The United States lean on to transport goods and pharmaceuticals? It was truck drivers and a few others in the transportation industry. There are hundreds of companies underpaying their drivers because they know some people are more likely to settle for the bare minimum instead of having nothing at all. Families and close friendships tend to fall apart due to the demanding work hours, requirements of a company, and limited communication between all parties. In this field, you have to be resilient, especially mentally, because between your driving hours, breaks, other drivers cutting you off, or receiving an inadequate amount of rest, this can cause you to experience burnout. If you are a trucker and have not heard this in a while, I am proud of you and appreciate you. If it were not for you, there would not be food, clothes, petroleum, nitrogen, toiletries, furniture, cars, etc., delivered across the world. Yes, it is true; TRUCKERS make the world go round not

automated trucks!

TRUCKING IS A MAN'S JOB...

SAYS WHO?

DEBRA M. FUSEINI

LYRICAL

PRESS

Contents

Introduction: Prosperity & Tranquility   1

Phase 1-Obtaining Licensure   6

    ➢ Class A CDL
    ➢ Endorsements
    ➢ Other Credentials

Phase 2-Selecting A Company   17

    ➢ Divisions
    ➢ Pick A Lane
    ➢ Training
    ➢ Equipment

Phase 3-Safety Is Top Priority   34

    ➢ Driving
    ➢ Trip Planning
    ➢ Protection

Phase 4-Embrace A Healthy Lifestyle   46

> ➤ Dietary Intake
> ➤ Exercising
> ➤ Hygiene
> ➤ Burnout

Phase 5-Enjoy The Ride   59

> ➤ Consistency
> ➤ Opportunities Prevail
> ➤ Stay Focused

Phase 6-Do Not Lose Yourself   72

Suggested Tips   76

Acknowledgements   80

About the Author   85

The best investment is investing in yourself. Many disregard the distinctions between external & internal confidence. It is imperative to own both…

Introduction

Prosperity & Tranquility

As a young woman standing big and tall at 5' 2, weighing about 124 pounds, I decided to take a leap of faith and join the trucking industry on June 17, 2017. "Awwwww, mane, what was I thinking?" Multiple thoughts scattered through my mind like an intricate maze I never created before. I began thinking about the world of trucking being predominantly "a man's world," with a steady increase in women embarking on this journey. The most significant factor, which crossed my mind, was my safety; "how will I protect myself if I need to?"

In the beginning, like many, I was puzzled yet tranquil while researching different schools on where to obtain my Class A-Commercial Driver's License known as a CDL. First, you contemplate, "why do I want to enter the trucking industry?" Next, figure out your goals and methods towards executing your plans effectively. Thirdly, choose whether you would prefer driving as a solo driver or if teaming with someone is a better option. Lastly, analyze the requirements affiliated in your state, which will permit you to receive your CDL as rules, and regulations vary from state to state.

This is not your typical DMV guide or new employee handbook exhibited from other resources. Instead, this informative piece will facilitate a brief understanding of what the trucking profession entails from a woman's perspective. Based on things I have encountered, I guide you through many levels of my career. There are different phases you will experience after you pass your licensing exam. You might hear, "trucking is not for everyone," or "trucking is a waste of life." To be successful, you have to be conscientious of your surroundings, reliable, patient, self-disciplined, and consistent.

Additionally, when interacting with individuals at truck stops, ports, shipping and receiving facilities, your communication skills play a pivotal role in determining your success. The truth is I had no idea where to start. Through these steps, you will learn and understand receiving your CDL can be quite simple, but the trucking industry will shape or break you.

Do what you love, love what you do, and do not allow discouragement to restrict you…

Obtaining Licensure

> ➢ Class A CDL

> ➢ Endorsements

> ➢ Other Credentials

So you made it! From analyzing multiple resources, you came across the right one. Here is what you need to know, there is no perfect resource or guide that will prepare you for what the world of trucking has in store. You have to experience the harassment, wait times at facilities, restless days and nights, losing close relationships, and other drivers jeopardizing your life by aggressive driving. One of the greatest tips in moving forward is remembering your purpose for trucking and keeping goals aligned with your endeavors. The best way to start is to obtain a CDL manual from your local DMV, and study at your own pace. You can choose to review the material and go to the DMV to take the class A CDL permit test or locate a school teaching you the information, and then go to the DMV to test for your permit.

Class A CDL

Although there are different classes of a license, your class A CDL indicates you can operate a gross vehicle weight rating

(GVWR) of 26,001 lbs or more. Testing typically includes general knowledge, air brakes, combination vehicle, and pre-trip inspection. This information is applicable for North Carolina, as it may be contingent in other states.

Several trucking schools will teach the fundamentals of pre-trip and post-trip inspections and backing maneuvers. You must find a school that is licensed, certified, or accredited.

- A licensed school will meet the state's standards through its facility, training, and course studies.
- The state licenses a certified institution; individuals from third

party organizations perform inspections on whether the school follows proper protocol. US DOT requirements must be met for students to graduate under this level.

- o An accredited school adheres to the rules and regulations indicated by the US Department of Education.

Even though a school may be deemed as licensed, accredited, or certified, please do your research on these establishments prior to attending. People ponder on a common question, "is it possible to get your CDL without going to school?"

Interestingly enough, the answer is yes, but it is more challenging getting on board with trucking companies due to inadequate training and experience. There may be a section when filling out applications inquiring about the school attended when receiving your CDL. These companies want to be sure you are hirable under specific standards. For instance, do not allow criminal or traffic convictions to impede you from getting a CDL as certain companies will accept you under their policies. Be cognizant of the significance of which route you choose to take when starting this process. Some of the biggest benefits that come with your class A CDL are endorsements.

Endorsements

Endorsements are classifications listed on your CDL, which permit you to transport hazardous materials, or liquid bulk items in a tank. If you want to pursue the division of hauling doubles and triples, be aware these trailers are about 28.5 feet long, connected by dollies, and the commodities do vary. Although endorsements are not required upon obtaining your CDL, they will open more job opportunities for you.

Companies such as FedEx, Landstar, and Airgas may qualify you as an eligible candidate based on these certifications. If you decide to get your endorsements, I recommend taking them around the time you test for your CDL to avoid multiple trips to the DMV.

From experience, VL Trucking, Inc., an over the road (OTR) carrier, did not make it a requirement to be hazmat endorsed upon hire. This company has dozens of hazmat contracts. They are susceptible to hiring drivers without the endorsement in hopes their drivers will test for it at some point. Through trial and error, you will figure out which division is more appealing based on pay, benefits, commodities, routes, time off, etc. It takes some drivers 2-3 companies before they realize whether hauling hazmat materials or transporting doubles and triples is most feasible.

Other Credentials

A passport is not necessary for many trucking companies, but it can be extremely beneficial for those places that haul freight between the United States, Canada, and Mexico. Furthermore, in situations when delivering or picking up loads from military bases, your passport is an alternative form of identification.

Next, the Transportation Worker Identification Credential, also known as a TWIC card, permits quicker access when arriving and departing from port facilities. Dozens of shipments are transported overseas. Many truck drivers find it useful to obtain a TWIC card because of less time spent during the check-in and out process.

The FAST pass, which stands for Free And Secure Trade, is a card allotted to truckers who do not exhibit high-risk issues. This card ensures faster access for truckers traveling from the USA into Canada and Mexico by utilizing FAST lanes.

Finally, Personal Protective Equipment (PPE) is mandatory at certain facilities for safety purposes. PPE often includes a hard hat, hearing protection, a high visibility vest, work gloves, safety boots, and safety glasses or goggles.

Although the materials listed above are not a requirement nor often discussed, they may further assist you throughout your trucking pursuits.

Once you understand your intrinsic value, a sound mind will permit you to make wiser decisions in life...

Selecting A Company

- ➢ Divisions
- ➢ Pick A Lane
- ➢ Training
- ➢ Equipment

It is vital when entering this profession you are conscientious yet knowledgeable of the different factors when choosing "your right" company. One major aspect to evaluate is your expectations when joining a trucking company.

It is important to question things, such as "how often do you want to go home, what type of benefits are offered, is there a healthy balance along with financial stability?" Moreover, do you want to be a company driver, lease a truck to own, or become an owner operator where you buy a truck and have more control over your business? There are many key pieces to scrutinize when selecting a company, but you can strategize where you choose to go based on the trucking industry's multiple divisions through research.

Divisions

Some trucking divisions include flatbed, step deck, oversized loads, car hauling, refrigerated, dry van, and tanker units. Upon researching different companies, focus on which division may best suit your needs. As a trucker, if inclement weather like hail, rainstorms, and scorching heat frustrates you, I highly recommend avoiding flatbed, step deck, oversize loads, and car hauling. When transporting refrigerated items, inconsistencies may arise during the times for picking up and delivering loads. If you are not prone to waking up and driving through a staggered pattern, this division might not be practical for you.

In regards to dry van companies, many operate from 7 am to 5 pm. Other common facilities under 24-hour operations are specific industrial plants such as Dow Chemical Co and distribution centers like

Target, Costco, and Wal-Mart. Once you figure out which division aligns with your path, thoroughly assess which is a better option when pursuing a lane.

Pick A Lane

Several companies offer local, over the road (OTR), regional, and dedicated accounts. For instance, you may apply for a local position at Total Wine. The company provides you with a day cab tractor (a truck without a bed), working from 4 am to 2 pm between Thursday-Monday. Your assigned route runs through a 250-mile radius from the Total Wine terminal in Albany, Georgia. This could include 7 to 11 stops at grocery stores throughout your shift. You will be responsible for unloading the crates of wine and documenting information from each stop under stressful circumstances, but the benefit allows you to be home every night.

On the bright side, not all local positions require you to unload freight because once you deliver; some third party affiliates have a role in unloading trucks. If local work sounds physically demanding, then try going OTR.

Most OTR companies prefer drivers to drive all 48 states, and some run into Canada and Mexico. You will be assigned a sleeper cab (a truck with a bed). Depending on the company, they expect their drivers to stay out between 2-3 weeks, 3-4 weeks, or

5-6 weeks. It is seldom you will deliver to the same place more than two or three times because companies tend to have many contacts in different states, so always prepare for a new adventure. OTR company drivers are normally paid by the mile; it could range from $0.21-$0.70 cents or more, whereas most local opportunities offer hourly rates.

As an OTR driver, you are less likely to unload freight; shipping and receiving facilities use their employees to load and unload trucks. If being away for a prolonged period bothers you, OTR will not be a suitable choice, and another area to consider is regional.

Regional accounts vary depending on the geographic region you are located. For example, if you reside in Bronx, New York, you may land a job at Threads Clothing factory by Zipporah. They will provide you with all the fundamentals needed to be successful, but they only service the Northeast region. The contract entails delivering to other affiliated clothing stores within that region. You might get home every other night or stay out three days at a time. This option is an excellent choice for someone who does not want to stray too far away from home.

Although going regional sounds like a breeze strolling through Central Park, analyze the overall region instead of the actual work. I assure you, ascending and descending through the mountains near Donners Pass in the Northwest during the winter season will differ from the inclines and declines traveling through Fancy Gap in the Northeast. Drivers, who are not content with the regional outlook, steer towards dedicated lanes.

Lastly, dedicated assignments align with a specific company such as Dollar General, Target, or Hobby Lobby. A trucking company in Houston, Texas, decides to hire you to work under a Dollar General account. Once you have your equipment, you are assigned to five stores in the Houston area, which you have to unload the freight, but you are home every night. If you demand specificity within your line of work, then dedicated contracts will be most comfortable for you.

The most common fields I have encountered are local and OTR. Before you decide where you want to train, understand many local gigs will not hire you as an inexperienced driver. These companies are more stringent with their hiring requirements and prefer you have at least six months to one year of OTR experience.

A local opportunity will permit you to be home frequently, but the work could be more strenuous, whereas some OTR companies require more time spent away from home, with less strain on your body.

All of these experiences can be rewarding but ultimately, whichever lane you choose, boils down to personal preference.

Training

I realized after I chose to go OTR; my biggest challenge was training. I was subjected to this male stranger in a confined area for 40 days and 40 nights, like how it rained in Noah's Arc. Individual companies have devised their unique platform for training. As a trainee, you will quickly determine whether this profession is practical for you during your training process.

After receiving my CDL certification from Carolina Truck Driving School in

Salisbury, North Carolina, I transitioned to Stevens Transport in Dallas, Texas. I chose Stevens due to its affiliation with the school I attended. Even though my training lasted six weeks long, I gained a sufficient amount of knowledge. Among various tasks, I learned how to back up a 70-80 feet truck safely. I acquired the skills to trip plan effectively, log hours of service, and understand the true importance of inspections with DOT officials (Department of Transportation).

You have to make the most of your training experience because your trainer has the most control in dictating whether you are eligible to move forward to work for that company. Some trainers value their position by teaching you as much as possible with reading an atlas, exiting ramps safely, sliding tandems, and switching lanes properly. You may receive a complacent trainer who does not instill foundational elements like backing up, logging information into your electronic device, or fueling.

When setting up preferences for your trainer, it is crucial to specify whether you prefer a male or female trainer, a smoker, or a non-smoker, and indicate any pet allergies. You will notice some trainers travel with their animals OTR. If you have more of a recluse personality, then training with a stranger in a confined space for hours, days, or weeks at a time could be mentally draining. If you are a social butterfly and it does not bother you to undergo such arrangements, your training will likely be enjoyable and comforting. Always remember to advocate for yourself and set reasonable boundaries. Training in a particular type of truck is a huge factor.

Equipment

Trucks come in different styles, shapes, and sizes. For someone of shorter stature, like 5'0", it is slightly challenging to see over the hood of a long nose Peterbilt 379 compared to a 579 model. The turn radius requires more caution with extended hoods. While waiting for your trainer, take the opportunity to research different trucks to facilitate your understanding of the equipment. Some companies you go to might only have Freightliner Coronados, Kenworth T680s, or Peterbilts. The inventory of other places could have Volvos, Internationals, or Mack trucks.

Two of the biggest components to consider are whether the trucks have a manual or automatic transmission. I place great emphasis on this because if you obtain your CDL in an automatic truck, you will have a restriction placed on your license prohibiting you from operating a manual transmission. Certain companies have automatic trucks while others have manuals, but it is better to attain the necessary skills in both areas.

Once you strategize wisely on companies that fit your criteria with equipment, ask yourself these few questions: "what are some of the necessities you need in a truck? Is not having a truck equipped with a fridge or microwave a deal-breaker? Do you need an inverter for plugging up devices like a laptop, TV, or radio? Are you someone who prefers many compartments due to your belongings?

Is there enough space for my pet to ride along comfortably? Will there be a second bunk bed for my brother or sister in case he or she decides to join on a few trips?" You will have a fair amount of questions that arise, but the key elements are a company's CSA (Compliance, Safety, and Accountability) score, reputability, credibility, and turnover ratio.

In trucking, nothing is ever guaranteed, so always plan strategically...

Safety Is Top Priority

> ➢ Driving

> ➢ Trip Planning

> ➢ Protection

Your commercial driver's license can be challenging to receive, but it is one of the easiest to lose. Imagine a group of high school students traveling southbound on I-10 heading towards San Diego, California, with a distracted driver on the phone. The entire time you are in the right lane, following alongside them at a safe distance while they are in the middle lane.

Unexpectedly, the driver swerves toward you because he misses his exit, causing a major accident where their car flips and your truck slams right into them as it continues to skid into other cars due to the impact and weight of your vehicle.

Highway Patrol and State Troopers arrive to assess the scene, immediately; they automatically assume the trucker is at fault. Situations like this will be out of your control, but having a dash camera will protect you from jeopardizing your career. You can never be too cautious.

Having your CDL comes with specific rules. For a professional truck driver to operate a commercial motor vehicle, it is critical to adhere to the Federal Motor Carrier Safety Administration (FMCSA). These guidelines will affect driving events, how you trip plan, and methods you use to protect yourself. A major concern for truck drivers is their safety. As a trucker, you have the ultimate control over what happens when you are behind the wheel but cannot accommodate someone else's actions in another vehicle.

Driving

It can be hectic driving for many truckers during 2-5 pm and 1-4 am due to various events. While driving in the afternoon around rush hour, it is pivotal you stay vigilant. When individuals are leaving work, many are in a hurry to head home or their next destination. You may notice more aggressive driving, tailgating, road rage, and drivers who are distracted by their phones.

Driving between 1-4 am, you will encounter nocturnal deers, drunk drivers, fatigue driving, or unaware drivers. The best and safest practices as a professional truck driver are maintaining following distance, checking your mirrors frequently, using your four-way flashers during hazards, and reducing while maintaining your speed, especially during inclement weather.

One of the most important pieces of advice is, DO NOT become complacent when driving your truck! Other methods that have contributed towards my success driving over the road are following "G.O.A.L," which stands for get out and look. In any backing event that you are unsure about, please GET OUT AND LOOK to gauge the entire perimeter before you complete your backing. I emphasize G.O.A.L because I have witnessed other drivers backing into cars, buildings, another truck at truck stops, shipping and receiving facilities, and ports only by not assessing their situation.

Another technique I value would be "midway inspections!" It is vital to check for any fluid or air leaks under the hood and inspect your tires after driving 250-350 miles. Sometimes if you go that duration without stopping for fuel, a meal, to stretch, or check your tires, you could be riding on a flat trailer tire and not even know. Once you become accustomed to or understand the "trucking lifestyle," you will realize planning your route is inevitable before you start driving.

Trip Planning

It is important to learn how to trip plan during your training phase. Trip planning includes interstates, US highways, and or local routes you will take from your shipper to receiver. Also, you need to plan where you will stop for fuel, showers, 30-minute and 10-hour breaks. During training, you may learn about the places that you want to avoid taking 34-hour resets to refresh your 70-hour working clock.

Due to FMCSA, new changes to the hours of service have been implemented over the years. Before reaching 8-hours of driving, it is required you take a 30-minute break. Once you have exceeded your driving hours for the day, which is 11-hours, a 10-hour break is needed to restore your working clock. There are 70-hours within your workweek. It is your discretion to do a 34-hour reset to restart your 70-hours. To bypass this reset, you have to be willing to drive at least 8 ½ hours or less a day. As a part of trip planning, many drivers reset at truck stops, hotels, or go home if possible. This is your time to rejuvenate, do laundry, or venture out and explore wherever you are located.

Trip planning effectively takes effort, time, and patience. For instance, if you are traveling from Maine to Nevada, then you want to be cognizant of the weather forecasts along the route. The more you trip plan, the better your transitions will be during transit. As part of your safety, plan your trips wisely and always remember to protect yourself at all times.

Protection

It can be nerve-racking over the road or even local, for a truck driver, because things happen that are out of your control. Between drunk drivers tailgating, or people firing their weapons while driving on the interstate, you must protect yourself at all times when you enter this industry. If you decide to engage with the wrong driver, your CDL, job, or life could be at stake.

You have to stay informed of state and local news events. A mass shooting could be going on in Oklahoma, where you are supposed to deliver. An explosion could have occurred along your route at a chemical plant in Texas where you were scheduled to pick up your next load. Your life should be the most valuable asset to you on the road, so consider preventive measures that could help you stay safe.

For those who are unaware, firearms are permitted in the trucking industry with stipulations. Certain motor carriers are against firearms as a part of their policy, so you can determine whether a company will be suitable for you under these terms and conditions. You are obligated to learn and understand when traveling between different states; they also have their own set of rules and regulations for truck drivers who carry firearms. Once you have all the necessary information in order, it is essential to follow proper protocol with a concealed permit and safely secure your weapon.

As a young woman in this profession, I have noticed other women drivers who prefer to team up with a partner, bring their pet along, or carry a pocketknife. Other forms of protection include a stun gun, taser, mace, pepper spray, or even wasp spray. Whichever method you choose, just make sure it works best for you.

Many individuals value money, but fail to realize you need your health to sustain your financial gains...

Embrace A Healthy Lifestyle

> ➢ Dietary Intake

> ➢ Exercising

> ➢ Hygiene

> ➢ Burnout

Trucking is a lifestyle you have to embrace because this is not an average 9-5 job at a marketing agency. The moment you obtain your CDL and start working for a trucking company your circumstances change. In the aspect of health and wellness, you may undergo extreme bodily changes that could affect your well-being.

There are dozens of assumptions about truck drivers' dietary intake, exercising habits, hygiene, and burnout.

One could project ideas that truckers are unhealthy due to some of the restaurants associated with truck stops and service plazas. Another assumption is truckers do not partake in physical activity nor maintain their appearance. One could even ask, "how is it possible for a truck driver to experience burnout when they're driving all the time?"

Dietary Intake

Upon entering this profession, you could have a petite and athletic build, weighing about 134lbs. After 14 months of encountering this lifestyle, it is a huge possibility your build could drastically change to husky and unfit, weighing about 264lbs. I strongly encourage you to be heedful of what you consume OTR or local because it could catch up to you. Some drivers prefer to cook in their trucks using countertop burners, crockpots, skillets, and deep fryers.

Others may purchase a George Forman grill, rice cookers, and electric kettles for boiling water. Improvising is necessary for the trucking industry, and you will soon learn the importance of maintaining your health on the road. Juicing can be essential for those who want to clear out their digestive system with the benefits of organic fruits and vegetables. Some people integrate beets, carrots, lettuce, celery, kale, etc. in a juicer to form a natural yet healthy concoction. Others who focus on fruits may create a mixture of kiwi, mangos, pineapples, grapes, apples, and bananas.

After driving 7 ½ to 9 hours a day, you might not have the energy to cook or there may be limited resources wherever you are located. Always be prepared for the unexpected when you are over the road. I highly propose having a truck equipped with an inverter or an auxiliary power outlet to plug up your items. Setting up meal plans, staying hydrated with water, taking vitamins, not consuming heavier meals before sleep, incorporating balanced fruits and vegetables in your diet will help you stay on a healthy track. Even though consuming the "right meals" is critical, exercising coincides with a healthy lifestyle on the road.

Exercising

Becoming a stagnant trucker could lead to not exercising regularly, especially if this was never a part of your routine. To avoid obesity, clogged arteries, sleep apnea, varicose veins, and much more, eat healthily and exercise often. If you can add at least 30-minutes of exercise to your daily regimen, do so as this will facilitate a healthier balance.

Along with your dietary intake, improvising will accommodate those who decide to formulate a workout routine in or around their truck. Some drivers, who are unable to go to the gym regularly, tend to lift weights, work on flexibility, enhance their coordination, or jog around the truck stop for 30-minutes. Depending on when you choose to exercise, you may notice slight changes in how you feel before, during, or after your driving shift. I often hear, "when you look good, you feel good," but this mainly pertains to your health; not solely, to what is aesthetically pleasing.

Some truckers adopt the ideology they cannot work out before or after drive shifts. Exercising habitually will help you perform better on the job as long as you are eager to change the quality of your thoughts. Your health is a top priority, and when you embark on this next journey in the trucking profession, you will quickly understand the value of exercising. People who are not "trucking inclined" have their own perception of a truck driver. There are days you may not be able to eat a good meal, exercise, or shower.

Hygiene

Have you ever stood in line while waiting to check-out and smelled such a pungent scent, which was nauseating coming from the person in front or behind you. Some truck drivers choose to shower once a week, twice a month, or every other month. Your hygiene contributes to a healthy balance on the road. If you do not take care of your skin and teeth, you could experience dermatitis neglecta, bacterial and fungal infections, or gum disease. You have the option of parking at truck stops, rest areas, or shipping and receiving facilities that permit overnight parking. If you decide to park in areas that do not suit all your needs, you may have to seek alternatives by brushing your teeth and cleaning yourself up inside your truck.

If your truck is not equipped with a shower, you can use a gallon of water; and some soap to wipe your body's essential areas. This option may not be ideal, but I guarantee you it is better than not washing at all. Your hygiene is another element that plays a crucial role as a trucker, and this will dictate whether the trucking industry is viable for you. This is a part of your everyday life, but without the proper balance, this job will take a toll on you.

Burnout

Many drivers exhibit burnout due to what the job entails. Physically, emotionally, mentally, and spiritually you will transition through the constant demands of OTR or local driving. You have drivers who drive 2,300-3,200 miles weekly and never go home for personal reasons. Others decide to drive 8-8 ½ hours a day consistently and choose not to take a 34-hour reset to refresh their 70-hour working clock.

Exhaustion can occur throughout different times from many events. As a trucker, you could be in traffic for 5 hours due to an accident or a hazardous incident on the interstate. Next, you might encounter inconsistent drive patterns reflecting delivery and pick up times from load assignments; or a receiver could reject your load, requiring you to drive 300 miles back to the shipper to return the freight; anything can happen.

When a driver has aspirations they are trying to achieve, minimize the amount of debt they have, or take care of their families back home, then feeling burnout will become inescapable. After you start generating the revenue that meets your standards, you will continue to strive for greatness in your divine way. Many companies want drivers to stay out as long as 3-5 weeks before taking time off. If you receive an opportunity to work somewhere that prefers their drivers to run 5 weeks at a time, I encourage you to make great use of your 34-hour resets and detox your body, mind, and soul.

To circumvent exhaustion safely, try to indulge in the great pleasures states have to offer, which you may not experience when you are home. You could go hiking in Denver, Colorado, sailing in Seattle,

Washington, exploring at The Metropolitan Museum of Art in New York, or relaxing in the sand in Miami, Florida. Do not neglect your health and burn yourself out to win your pursuits.

Certain distractions limit your ability to stay focused on important tasks...

Enjoy The Ride

- ➤ Consistency

- ➤ Opportunities Prevail

- ➤ Stay Focused

The 1st year of your trucking journey will be intriguing because whether you choose the local route, OTR, dedicated or regional accounts, you will notice changes in yourself. Your health, mood, and internal drive could shift dramatically. Consistency will attest to your positive results in this profession, and it will lead to new beneficial opportunities.

Many drivers implement different strategies towards achieving their goals. It will not always be simple, but tackling new challenges could present great rewards. What is baffling and unfortunate is some trainees do not exceed past 30, 60, or 90 days without quitting. Some complain the work is too demanding, while others get frustrated when presented with complex backing situations. Newer drivers do not know how to combat the feeling of loneliness OTR; instead of figuring out alternatives, they quit and go home.

As a woman in this industry, you cannot be oblivious or gullible when walking through truck stops and rest areas late at night. Some women do not excel due to trusting the wrong people, experiencing harassment, or driving in the wrong areas without being aware; you must stay vigilant. Some people feel like trucking is a man's job, but if you are willing to put in the same amount of work, then no one can tell you otherwise.

Consistency

The objective for many drivers after receiving their CDL is to work local positions so they can be home often. For local jobs, hundreds of companies will not hire you as a new driver unless you have at least one year of OTR experience. If you are consistent with your first trucking company, you will be able to expand your horizon with new offers.

There are local companies that will hire you upon graduating from CDL school, but the work could be arduous. Being consistent at your company will help you establish more rapport and longevity. Your employment history will follow you when venturing into your next opportunity, so evaluate what you truly want, and stick with it. Typically, after you work for a company for one year, your pay increases, and you may be eligible to receive various incentives they offer. What you may find challenging OTR are inconsistencies with your delivery and pick up times of your load assignments.

If you are working with a company that hauls refrigerated freight, be mindful these warehouses normally receive products between midnight and 8 am. Your dispatcher could assign your next load not temperature controlled, leading you to pick it up at noon, which may not deliver until the next day by 3 pm. Your drive shifts will vary, but you should always advocate if you are uncomfortable performing the job duties. You have to be functional to drive in the day and at night at all times, so make sure you receive an adequate amount of rest when time permits.

Opportunities Prevail

Opportunities will prevail when you have acquired the skills and gained enough experience after your first year, so enjoy the ride. There are resources and websites, such as glassdoor.com, simplyhired.com, indeed, and craigslist that you can utilize to search for your next opportunity in trucking. Most people are unaware of the staffing agencies, solely for drivers, which exist. As long as you have an idea of what you want in trucking, doors will open for you.

When I was training with Stevens Transport, I knew what I wanted financially after my first year. As my first year was approaching, I researched multiple companies, but none met my requirements; now, I felt in control. One late afternoon before I started driving, I searched on Craigslist, and miraculously, I found what met my expectations, VL Trucking, Inc. in Des Plaines, Illinois. They were a smaller carrier with less than 200 drivers, family-oriented, communication with dispatchers was fluid, and the pay was just what I needed. There was one setback; I needed more preparation. Although it was not a requirement to have your hazmat endorsement, your pay would increase abundantly.

After obtaining my CDL, I took the test for my endorsements at the same time to avoid returning to the DMV, so this was not disconcerting to me. My goal was to stay at my first company for about a year, and even though Stevens Transport provided me with phenomenal training, I wanted more financial stability. I went through proper procedures to secure hazmat loads and follow certain guidelines during DOT inspections. It is very important to know and understand as a driver, you may encounter a DOT inspection due to random selection, your trucking company, what is being transported, issues with clearance, or exceeding the weight limit.

DOT officials may target companies hauling hazardous materials because there are so many risks associated when not adhering to the protocols. Therefore, do what you are supposed to do to ensure others' safety and yourself when placarding your trailer and securing your load. Whichever division you enter, remain focused.

Stay Focused

Stay focused on what you are trying to accomplish. There will be sacrifices made towards relationships, friendships, and other connections established before trucking. Before you enter the trucking industry, those close to you may not understand why you decided to drive trucks, considering the negative connotations. You may hear about brutal attacks on truckers, or their equipment undergoes vandalism; a driver's health is the first thing to go, or it is easy to become lost within yourself as a driver.

Even though there is some truth to these statements, you are the sole individual controlling your focus. Under various circumstances, situations may arise in this profession, causing you to deviate from your focus, but being mentally resilient and remembering why you started your trucking journey tends to help your purpose come into existence through your reality.

Other things that may facilitate a strong focus: having a solid support system, knowledgeable mentors, meditation, and eliminating distractions. If you have younger children and you are the sole provider for your family, having a support system is especially important if you go over the road. Being over the road has its challenges, so your work life is less likely to be compromised when you have support from a distance.

Mentorship is a great way to become successful in the trucking industry. After you gain some experience and knowledge, you will decipher who you want as a mentor. Always be aware of where you receive your information because the worst thing about mentorship is being steered in the wrong direction by someone who also obtained inadequate information. Once you declutter your mind, dismiss anything that jeopardizes your position, and exclude things that hinder you internally, your focus will be much sharper.

There is this quote by an unknown source, "starve the distractions and feed the focus." Once you eliminate the things that are not serving your purpose, your focus will be enhanced at a higher magnitude. You will less likely get distracted at truck stops, incidents on the road, or other drivers who think they know everything. These distractions do not serve you, so remain focused.

If you are fearful and unable to compartmentalize your thoughts and emotions, trucking may be your worst enemy...

Do Not Lose Yourself

Most will contemplate on what "do not lose yourself" actually means. Indeed, many individuals misconceive the perception versus the reality of what the trucking industry entails. You will be in a confined area throughout your shift. Unless you are teaming with a partner, you could experience loneliness, resulting in changes to your personality or quitting your job. If you tend to seclude or isolate yourself in this profession and cannot balance your thoughts and emotions, you may be at a higher risk of losing yourself. I assure you, there is much more to this industry besides "put it in gear and go."

Key things to notate aside from being a professional driver, you will encounter pre-trip and post-trip inspections on your own and along with DOT officials. Some may find this impossible, but if you fall susceptible to neglecting a healthy lifestyle, you may undergo the ramifications of deteriorating health. On some days, due to complacency, carelessness, or laziness, you might stop brushing your teeth, or even showering. Your appearance and body odor play a key role in the possible interactions with associates at shipping, receiving, and truck stop facilities.

This line of work can be demanding, with driving long hours and not balancing your resting cycles. Although it can be strenuous at times, always remember you are the most valuable to the trucking profession, so do not forget who you are and why you started this journey. There will be people you have known all your life, which those relationships may no longer be of existence because of the time spent away from home.

Many drivers end up losing their families, homes, vehicles, and investments. Communication is a major component in relationships; therefore, maintain consistency with those most significant in your life. Due to this job's higher stress levels, truckers are exposed to multiple personalities at facilities, other reckless drivers, issues with equipment, and pressure exhibited from their companies.

Some drivers begin to develop negative habits such as tailgating, cell phone use, chain-smoking, and drinking alcohol during work shifts. Based on the amount of stress and habits created, you might steer down the wrong path trying to escape reality. This industry requires a great deal of patience compared to other fields. If you dive into this opportunity, always remember your purpose and goals aligned with your path.

Suggested Tips

+ Complacency can be crippling, so have a blueprint before you start trucking!
+ Be financially prepared when you begin this new experience!
+ Research substantially on the CDL school & company you choose for training!
+ Find a training company that allows only one trainer & one trainee on a truck!
+ If you decide to team, try teaming with someone of familiarity, but set boundaries before moving forward!
+ Stay updated & alert with local weather & news events along your route!

- As a woman, when exploring salons, galleries, or restaurants on your 34-hour reset, remain vigilant!
- Google load facilities before arrival to assess the perimeter!
- Keep your load accommodations to yourself to avoid any mishaps on the road!
- Invest in a CB radio to communicate with other truckers regarding any incidents or accidents on the road!
- Always use your four-way flashers to indicate hazards ahead for drivers behind you who are unable to see!
- For security purposes, utilize a tracking app with someone you confide in & always lock your doors!

- If you carry a firearm in your truck, please be conscientious of the rules & regulations in each state!

- Not all US HWYs are truck friendly; avoid US HWY 33 & US HWY 6 especially at night!

- If you drive at night, consider "midway inspections" on your truck!

- During transit, when deers approach your vehicle at night, use a deer whistle or your air horn; your headlights or high beams will blind them!

- When someone is backing up their truck, patience is a virtue!

- A tire pressure gauge is a great tool to have, but check your mirrors frequently during transit!

- The "what-if scenario," such as having an idea of what will happen before it occurs during travel & maintaining following distance, will cause fewer incidents or accidents!
- Situations involving right turns at traffic lights, tend to be safer when you turn on green!
- If you're late or rude with shippers & receivers, get ready to wait!
- In trucking especially, your instincts are normally right!
- If necessary, bring your dog, cat, rabbit, or parrot on the road!

Acknowledgments

I cannot have this piece completed without an abundance of thanks to the most high. Yes, indeed without GOD in my life, I feel inadequate, desolate, and astray. When traveling alone, and there is no conversationalist available, I call on the most high and always feel at peace. From the moment I started this new experience, I kept second-guessing myself on making the right decision.

I contemplated my health, safety, and finances. Entering the trucking industry with predominantly men and limited guidance, the main source I leaned towards was GOD. When I received my CDL and made it through my training successfully, it felt like an anchor was lifted off my shoulders, and I was ready to roll on my own.

Now, this may sound egotistical or even arrogant, but I thank myself for not allowing others who discouraged me from pursuing my endeavors. From family to friends to associates, everyone had their opinion on what I should do with my life, but I lived up to my expectations through confidence and a dash of faith. I made countless mistakes, even ones no one knows but GOD. The mistakes and failures I learned from have shaped me into someone a lot stronger and wiser.

Words cannot describe my gratitude for this one individual. We started establishing rapport during the earlier stages of our trucking careers. He is logical, intelligent, determined, and a natural-born hustler. KayBee Tha Trucker is someone who challenged me through my experience. Have you ever met someone who instantly believed, encouraged, and supported you, yet you were still strangers to each other? Well, he believed in me the way I believe in myself; this is what made me gravitate towards him. As I previously mentioned, those closest to me were not too fond of the idea of me driving trucks, but his hope and faith in me gave me more assurance that I could conquer anything I put my mind to.

As for my social media platform, those who have shown a tremendous amount of support through YouTube, Instagram, or email, you are phenomenally amazing, and I thank you from the heart. Although I can be "stubborn," thank you Ted for training me; John simply for your consistency, and King Drodge for the different perspectives you always provided.

Most significantly, I thank my parents because without them, I would not have made it this far in life nor be the woman I am today. I am grateful for all the lessons, blessings, and discipline. Mother always said, "Train up a child the way they should go, and when they grow up, they won't depart from it; humility before honor."

To my beautiful siblings Ohemaa, Kissiwaa, and Boatemaa, "hmmm…we came a long way right, yeah I know!" Growing up in our household with so many restrictions, yet blissful memories was a blessing. Ohemaa, you always stood by me regardless of certain circumstances trying to mold me into a better woman and I thank GOD I had someone stronger to look up to. A delicate uniqueness about each of you pushes me to exceed my expectations. Whether it deals with parenting, academics, or organic artistry, the ambition you all possess entices me, and I will always be proud of all of you. Thank you for being patient with me!

About The Author

Born to Ghanaian parents in New York but raised in North Carolina, an ambitious woman overflowing with ideas that only an adrenaline junkie could understand the need to have such ideas manifested. After the 7th grade, my school academics took a spiraling turn like a tornado traveling at 74mph, mind boggling.

Constantly, trouble prevailed with the rebellious and carefree personality I had during those times. I only went to college to redeem and prove myself wrong that I could achieve anything I put my mind to. I attended Northern Virginia Community College and received an Associates degree in General studies; I was thankful I graduated Cum Laude. Thereafter, I obtained my Bachelors in Sociology and minors in Social Welfare and Psychology at Virginia Commonwealth University.

At the time, I envisioned a social service and advocacy organization facilitating the needs of at-risk children and adolescents. Due to inexperience and multiple rejection letters and emails, I did not have the proper credentials to be hirable by social service agencies.

After frustration, contemplating, and deliberating, I always wondered what it would be like to drive big trucks down the road. Obtaining my CDL was one of the biggest and best investments of my life.

Three years later, the liberation I feel over

the road is unmatched and priceless.

My life is what I choose to make it, &
there is nothing more promising than
that! Growth is inevitable, and once you
think you know everything, then it is time
to take a break from the truck!